Sea Salt Fertilization

Healthier Soil
and a Healthier You!

Eryn Paige

Green Eagle
publishing

Copyright Notice
Terms of Use & Disclaimer

Published by
Green Eagle Publishing

Special Terms of Use:
Disclaimer: *Sea Salt Fertilization - Healthier Soil and a Healthier You!* is not intended to be a prescription for the user. This book does not offer medical advice and its content has not been evaluated by the US Food and Drug Administration. It simply presents educational information regarding the exceptional benefits from using *good* sea salt to better feed the soil and plants. No information or products described in this book should be relied upon to diagnose, treat, cure, or prevent disease.

Resources will be shared which you can easily access for specific guidance on how to use the sea salt as an effective fertilizer. And *How to Grow Glorious Wheatgrass at Home Tutorial - With Salty Sea Mineral Eco-Fertilization for Superior Mineral Rich Soil* by Eryn Paige contains detailed information for applying sea salt fertilization to wheatgrass.

HealthBanquet.com, LLC

Table of Contents

About the Author

Eryn Paige, Editor of HealthBanquet.com, enjoys researching and educating on nature's bounty that is available to keep us healthier and happier on planet Earth. She has also written *How to Grow Glorious Wheatgrass at Home Tutorial - With Salty Sea Mineral Eco-Fertilization for Superior Mineral Rich Soil.* In experimenting with growing wheatgrass, she realized the tremendous benefits of fertilizing with sea salt and felt this very important subject deserved a book of its own.

Visit the Author at:
www.healthbanquet.com
www.facebook.com/healthbanquet

After you have read this book, please leave an Amazon review. I hope you will pass along this message so more and more people will implement it in their gardens and farms leading to healthier soil and lives.

Also by Eryn Paige
How to Grow Glorious Wheatgrass at Home Tutorial - With Salty Sea Mineral Eco-Fertilization for Superior Mineral Rich Soil

How and Why to Make Divine Soaked Flour Bread – For Easier Digestion and Optimized Nutrition

Dedication, Gratitude, Preface

Dedication and Acknowledgement: *Sea Salt Fertilization - Healthier Soil and a Healthier You!* is dedicated to those interested in organic gardening and farming, sustainability, wanting to minimize the use of dangerous chemical fertilizers, pesticides, and herbicides, and to those desiring healthier soil, plants, animals, and people.

It is also dedicated in memory of Dr. Maynard Murray, author of *Sea Energy Agriculture. He* was a true pioneer in mineral rich, unrefined, "sea salt" fertilization and dedicated his life to this subject and to spreading the word about it. Additionally, this book is dedicated in memory of Charles Walters, author of *Fertility From The Ocean Deep*. When growing wheatgrass and seeing firsthand how positively the wheatgrass was responding to sea salt, I started researching and came across those two books on the subject of fertilizing with "sea salt." Both of these men have passed away. I hope the dedication and work on this subject has not been in vain, and that the day will come when "sea salt fertilization" is *widely* used around the world. Through my book, I hope to bring further attention to this topic. The *time is now* for earth-friendly sea energy agriculture to be widely implemented.

Gratitude: Tremendous gratitude to my husband, Mark—my true hero, my insightful mother for her many good ideas, and to my precious family and friends who continually inspire me.

Preface: Mineral and trace element rich good sea salt addresses nutrient deficiency in the soil. Soil with inadequate minerals, grows plants that are unable to uptake all the minerals they genetically can. Nutrient depleted soil leads to malnourished plants and people. Eating foods grown in mineral depleted soils do not meet the mineral needs of the body. Much unwellness and disease can be attributed to a mineral deficiency. Consequently, remineralizing our soil can positively impact our foods and health.

My idea to use sea salt with growing wheatgrass came from my experiences using it in my kitchen. I soaked walnuts occasionally in a sea salt solution and then dehydrated them to help neutralize their enzyme inhibitors, thus making them easier to digest, and sometimes added them to my popular homemade bread recipe in *How and Why to Make Divine Soaked Flour Bread – For Easier Digestion and Optimized Nutrition* at my website HealthBanquet.com.

I knew sea salt had antifungal and antibacterial properties—helping to prevent the growth of bacteria in the soaking fluid. At first, I was having much difficulty growing my wheatgrass. Since the sea salt and water was of benefit with the soaking process for walnuts, I thought that it might be beneficial for soaking my wheatgrass seeds in too.

To my delight, I noticed a tremendous increase in the vitality of my wheatgrass. I began wondering how this "magic" sea salt could have such a profound impact on its growth. I experimented more and was very encouraged with the results. This led me to dig deeper into the subject and I'd like to share with you what I've learned. I also wrote *How to Grow Glorious Wheatgrass at Home Tutorial - With Salty Sea Mineral Eco-Fertilization for Superior Mineral Rich Soil.*

My goal for this book is to further spread the word on sea salt fertilization to *ideally* foster a worldwide movement. I want to communicate that whole, mineral and trace element abundant sea salt is a tremendous ally to us—we are doomed without salt! For good, mineral rich, whole, *non-refined* sea salt, *in the right amount*, is tremendously valuable to us and is, in fact, necessary for our very existence. Our internal fluids are saline and all creatures require salt for their very survival.

Additionally, our precious little amount of land suitable for farming and gardening is quickly becoming devoid of minerals and trace elements. Many of humankind's "solutions" have only created more problems. But God in His all knowing, patient, forgiving and loving nature has awakened us, and, at the last minute as is so often the case, to a natural solution that has been there all along and is amply provided—good sea salt. I strongly believe properly utilizing the ocean's water will provide tremendous benefits for the health of soil, plants, animals, humans, and our planet.

Remember, it is imperative we pay close attention to Mother Nature and the wisdom she imparts. Let's learn more on the importance of good mineral abundant soil, the amazing health of marine life in non-polluted salty seawater, and how good "sea salt" can improve our soil, plants, and thus health. You will also learn about my favorite "sea salt" fertilizer and even how I used it to address hundreds of hungry caterpillars devouring a grapevine in my yard.

We have been blinded to this supreme ancient natural solution. It is time we take the blinders off, and *truly realize* how the seawater and its sea salt can come to the rescue. It is time to recognize and celebrate the goodness of mineral rich sea salt. It is time to embrace and incorporate the ocean's sea salt nutrients into the food chain on land—for a much healthier tomorrow to all who "live off the land!"

Thank you for reading my book! I hope this book leads to improvements with your "green thumb" and to changes that will make you and planet Earth healthier.

Chapter 1: Seawater and its Sea Salt – Friend or Foe?

"All truth passes through three stages. First, it is ridiculed. Second, it is violently opposed. Third, it is accepted as being self-evident."

—*Arthur Schopenhauer*

"Sea Salt is Good for Plants" - You Must Be Kidding Me!

Certainly everyone has heard how bad and undesirable salt is for our soil. That is certainly what I used to think. That was before I learned about the differences between salts and learned how to use "sea salt" to successfully grow wheatgrass.

Now that I have personally witnessed and seen firsthand how sea salt can help to grow healthier wheatgrass, I would like to share my experiences to open your mind to its true salty greatness.

I wonder how I can best communicate in a way to draw much needed attention to what I consider to be a phenomenal food source for soil and plants. How can I best communicate that plants fortunate enough to be "fed" these ocean minerals are healthier and more nutritious for us—from being given the opportunity to uptake the minerals they want from the sea salt enriched soil? How can I best shine further light on the potential of unrefined, whole sea salt that has been carefully harvested and solar dehydrated? I'll just do my best to communicate to you why I've found sea salt to be a phenomenal and highly nutritious gift.

First, I will share my success with using it to grow healthier wheatgrass. And, by sharing that success, I hope you, dear reader, will then ask yourself obvious questions... Can sea salt grow *other* healthier plants that are more vital and less susceptible to disease? Can sea salt revitalize our soil on a grand scale? Just *what else* can sea salt help us with?

I hope your eyes will be opened to the great potential of good sea salt. After you have read my book, I hope you will think that ocean salt can tremendously benefit soil, plants, and people through its powerfully nourishing and at the same time pest deterring qualities. And maybe you will also think that with using sea salt as an earth-friendly fertilizer, dangerous chemicals that damage us and the earth can be minimized.

How I Love Sea Salt, Let Me Count the Ways

I love seawater and its derivative sea salt. I love seaside vacationing. I love experimenting with sea salt. I eat sea salt. I bathe in sea salt. I grow plants with sea salt. I even like to do facials with sea salt.

When the neighborhood children come over, they are not surprised to see a huge variety of different salts in little bowls on my counters. They have a great time tasting the differing salts and remarking on their favorites. "Oh, this one tastes just like the ocean," says one. Another one remarks, "This one is the best!"

> **"The cure for anything is salt water: sweat, tears or the sea."**
> —Isak Dinesen

I was getting together with my good friend Toni recently. I was talking with her about sea salt being used for a fertilizer. I told her I was writing a separate book to bring more attention to just how valuable sea salt is for growing plants. As we were conversing about salt and the ocean, she told me the following story about the healing powers of the ocean that she remembers hearing from her mother Sophia.

"My mother Sophia was the first generation to be born in the United States from Greek immigrants who immigrated through Ellis Island in the early 1900s. Sophia's parents, James and Fani, brought to the United States all of their traditions that they had experienced in the Peloponnesus and Constantinople.

"One of these traditions when they lived in Greece was to go to the beach when they felt poorly. Once they moved to the Los Angeles area, they continued this tradition. They would go to the beach for their aches and pains, a common cold, for respiratory problems or to "heal the soul." Every Sunday after church, they'd all pack up and head for the beach and sometimes spend the night.

This beautiful sunset view is on the Southern California coast and is one of the beaches where Sophia and her family used to go.
Photograph by Al Alicea, AlAliceaPhotography.com.

"Living close to the beach turned out to be a godsend because Sophia contracted Polio when she was 14-years-old in the late 1930s.

"They would especially go to the beach on extremely hot days. They would throw down blankets on the sand and spend the night to avoid the heat. Again, my YiaYia (Greek for grandma) thought that this was very therapeutic in more ways than one. Whether it was the ocean air, saltwater, or salty sand, the ocean was used as a cure-all for everything.

"They would eat, drink, make merry and inhale the refreshing ocean air like it was going out of style. If one of them had a skin condition, they would sit at the end of the shore and let the waves cover them with their healing powers.

"Besides for Polio, Sophia also had Scarlet Fever and came out pretty much unscathed. The doctors told my grandmother that Sophia's prognosis was not good, and that she would surely end up in a wheelchair by the age of 30.

"Well, my mother did not end up in a wheelchair. Her parents' knowledge of the ocean's healing powers got her through the most difficult times. She just survived the Polio through the years, putting up with the aches and pains that came with it. She also lived through the Scarlet Fever. And she was VEEEEEERY proud of the fact that she NEVER, NOT ONCE took ANY prescribed medicine at ANY time in her life.

"Sophia went on to live a very active life, camping at local beaches well into her 70s, taking brisk hikes and setting up/breaking camp, walking five miles a day into her early 80s while leading her walking group decades younger than her, telling them to "pick up the pace," and lived until she was 10 days shy of her 87th birthday!"

The ocean and its salty composition is an amazing gift to humankind!

In this book, I shall communicate to you that sea salt is indeed *our friend* when used properly. I believe there is so much more we have to learn about the health aspects of the ocean. For now, let's start with learning more about sea salt and how it helped me to grow healthier wheatgrass.

Chapter 2: Wheatgrass Growing Challenges Abound Before Using Sea Salt as Fertilizer

"In *Eco-Farm, An Acres U.S.A. Primer*, it was settled without fear of contradiction that plants in touch with balanced nutrition, with a full variety of trace minerals, create their own hormone and enzyme potentials and therefore protect themselves against bacterial, fungal, viral and insect attack. Much the same is true for human beings."

—Charles Walters
Fertility From The Ocean Deep

Before Using Sea Salt for Wheatgrass Growing, Mold, Fungus, Sickly Looking, Poor Germination Experienced

When I first started growing wheatgrass, before using the nourishing good sea salt combined with water as a fertilizing mixture, I struggled for years with periodic mold, fungus, and sickly looking wheatgrass with inconsistent germination rates. I was able to grow nice looking wheatgrass before using the sea salt, however, my on-again-off-again challenges with problematic wheatgrass came to an end after using the good sea salt and water solution, and the wheatgrass looked much more vital.

Following are some pictures of the more disappointing results I had before using sea salt.

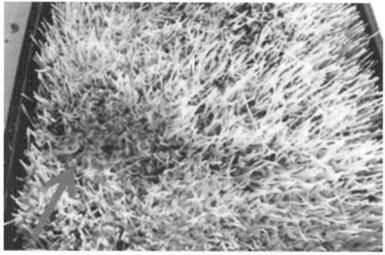

Mold sets in when germination falters.

It was difficult for me to *consistently* grow healthy looking wheatgrass. I tried various fertilizers and techniques, but it was not until I experimented with using sea salt, that my growing troubles were over.

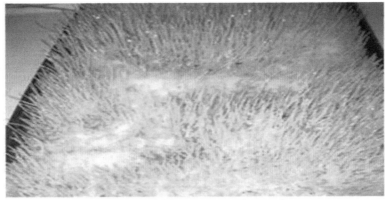

White cotton-like mold has overtaken wheatgrass tray.

Through the implementation of the sea salt and water fertilizing solution, I observed that *healthy* seeds and plants are better able to resist disease and fight off pathogens. I also learned that when something is wrong or out of balance with wheatgrass, the plant becomes perfect prey for pathogens, and for mold to take over.

Overall, before using a sea salt and water solution, the maturing wheat seeds were much more sensitive to imperfect growing conditions. The wheatgrass and seeds communicated their dissatisfaction to me visually by their sickly looking state.

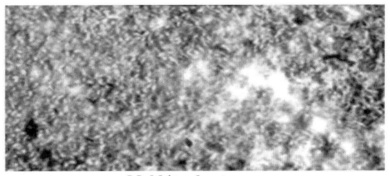

Mold in wheatgrass.

My frustrations with growing wheatgrass were later over with sea salt to the rescue....

Diluted "Seawater" Grows Healthier Wheatgrass

Wheatgrass being watered with sea salt diluted with water—like diluted seawater.

Wheatgrass flourishes when fertilized with sea salt and water formula.

Big challenges with poorly growing wheatgrass vanish. Succulent wheatgrass is result.

Sea salt "food" grows beautiful wheatgrass.

Once I incorporated sea salt into the growing process, my "happier" and healthier wheatgrass experienced:

- Richer, darker green blades

- Wider tipped blades exuberantly reaching for the sun

- Minimal to no mold or fungus

- No smell of grass or any particular scent—until harvested and juiced

- Juicier looking

- Sweeter, less bitter, more palatable taste

If you are interested in growing wheatgrass, I urge you to read my *How to Grow Glorious Wheatgrass at Home Tutorial* for step-by-step instructions.

Now that I've demonstrated the benefits of adding sea salt water to my wheatgrass, let's get a better understanding of what comprises these salts.

Chapter 3: Miraculous Ocean is an Organized Masterpiece of Chemical Elements

"Every disease is a sign of a lack of certain chemical elements. No disease can exist unless there is a lack of chemical elements in the body."

—Bernard Jensen
The Healing Power of Chlorophyll from Plant Life

90 Plus Naturally Occurring Elements in Periodic Table of Elements Exist in Ocean's Amazing Broth

The basic building blocks of everyday matter and of the universe are elements. *Everything* around you, every single natural and man-made thing you can see, every tree, pebble, plant, animal, and car is made up of elements. And we are made up of elements too. *Everything* inside of us is made up of elements. We truly are what we eat! Indeed, human life would be nothing without these elements.

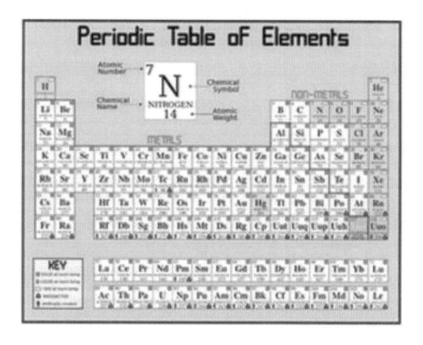

What is really something is that these elements that make up all life, 90 plus naturally existing chemical elements from our Periodic Table of Elements, are all found in a brilliantly organized and *liquefied* state in the water of our lively oceans. Again, 100% of the natural elements found on Earth, and that also happen to make up and support life, are found in the seawater—*each and every one of them*. The ocean water is a true storehouse and unique blend of the full spectrum of minerals and trace elements.

And our ocean life "bathes" and is perfectly nourished from this marvelously balanced saline solution. No fertilizing agents, pesticides, insecticides, herbicides, or medicines need to be added to the ocean for the life within to *superbly* thrive and be protected from disease.

Research was conducted in the 1930s revealing sea life with *extraordinary* health *and seemingly no signs* of cancer, arthritis, arteriosclerosis, and other aging factors.

Do you think we should be questioning just what nutritional ocean water "recipe" could be responsible for such a state of wellness in our sea life? Do you think we should be asking how we can best duplicate the wellness promoting qualities of our vast oceans and best provide this nourishing buffet for our land life too? How come only the sea creatures get this perfect banquet of minerals and trace elements?

With the many severe health challenges and diseases plaguing societies today, especially in the United States, do you think there should be front page news covering the outstanding health of the marine life when existing in non-contaminated waters? Should there be discussions on what we can learn from this?

Could it be the *perfect* combination of minerals and trace elements present in the ocean water are the *ideal* solution for the growth and support of both sea plants *and* land plants (given the right salinity); and subsequently, *tremendously* beneficial to those who eat these foods? I believe so.

Is there a way to "transfer" the ocean's "wellness promoting factor," its superb nutritive mineral and trace element content, so it can be used to *also* promote life, nourishment, and support to our soil and plants? The good news is that yes, after the ocean water is dehydrated, the ocean's liquid minerals "gather together" into the *solid* and slightly moist grains of sea salt. In other words, when seawater evaporates, its bountiful nutrients are left in the salt, so this good sea salt is the best known and easiest way, other than drinking seawater, to get all these nutrients.

This excellent salt can then be packaged and distributed. And this sea salt can then marvelously later feed soil and plants.

Why Does Good Soil Really Matter?

Growing wheatgrass taught me so many valuable lessons. And one was just how truly important it is to have good soil. Growing wheatgrass caused me to look quite differently at our grasslands.

Healthy looking cows grazing on grass in Wisconsin.

When visiting Wisconsin, I noticed the beautiful health of cows dining on fresh grass. Their coats were shiny and they seemed more "perky." I also noticed their "manure" appeared far healthier than from cows in feedlots!

> **"When the pasture provides appropriate nutrition, veterinary bills—except for trauma—virtually disappear."**
> —Charles Walters

The better the fertility, or immune system of the precious soil, the better the immune system of the grass or plant, and therefore, the better the immune system of the animal or human.

Both the human immune system and the plant immune system are *fundamentally* **interdependent on the nutrient quality and fertility of**

the soil. Our immune system, and *even our physical structure*, are a reflection of the foods we have eaten from either toxic and nutrient depleted soils, or wonderfully fertile soils.

Poor grass will endure, but nutrient rich grass produces champions. **And animals can graze on beautiful looking grass and yet still be in a starving situation because the visually misleading grass is actually deficient from its poverty stricken soil.**

Race horses in Kentucky are known to be incredibly sturdy and fast from eating bluegrass from calcium rich soil—minerals pass from soil, to grass, to the horses.

If the minerals and trace elements are all supplied in the soil, the plant will be able to extract what it wants. If they are absent from the soil, the plant will be unable to absorb that particular mineral or element.

Healthy mineral rich soil, good foods from that soil, and good health are *intimately* and strongly related.

A plant grown in poor soil, *may* look healthy and taste OK, but it can still be nutrient deficient. Each plant has different capabilities in terms of the types and amounts of minerals they can absorb from the soil.

Again, mineral deficient plants can look good but still be lacking in certain minerals because the minerals they would have liked to take in, simply were not in the soil for them to access. Beauty alone is not an indication that a plant absorbed all the minerals it wanted. Plants can still grow even though the soil is low in minerals. However, these mineral deficient plants are weaker, less healthy, and more susceptible to disease. On the other hand, a better more mineral rich "diet" equals better health for both plants *and* humans.

On average, plants extract about 40 elements from the soil—*only if they exist in the soil*. Each plant has different capabilities in terms of how many different minerals it can absorb. **Unfortunately, most commercial fertilizers add a *maximum* of six minerals back to the soil which can be inadequate and create imbalances.**

Here is an example regarding sweet potatoes. One sweet potato is grown in poor soil with just a few minerals, and another sweet potato is grown in soil with a full selection of minerals. Through testing, the mineral content of the sweet potato can be determined. And the sweet potato in the nutrient poor soil may be shown to only contain 10 – 15 minerals. However, the sweet potato grown in the soil with all mineral and trace elements provided can be tested and shown to have 56 minerals. Which sweet potato would you rather eat and which one is most nutritious?

A *wide* variety of minerals are *essential* to the proper functioning of man. *In time*, more will be learned on how *all* the minerals in the atomic table benefit man on some level.

> **"Eliminate deficiency and you eliminate the disease."**
> —Charles Walters

Let's learn about the health of ocean life in unpolluted waters.

Chapter 4: Why is Marine Life so Healthy and What Can We Learn From This?

"Stay close to nature and its eternal laws will protect you."
—Dr. Max Gerson

Can We "Capture" Positive Essence of Ocean for Agriculture

Dr. Murray was one of the researchers largely intrigued with the ocean and its significant positive health impact on sea life. He was a former physician and physiologist, and author of *Sea Energy Agriculture*. He was *in awe* from witnessing the *unsurpassed* health of the flourishing marine life.

Marine life in clean seawater is found to be in superior health.
Photograph by Al Alicea, AlAliceaPhotography.com.

"Sometimes we are lucky enough to know that our lives have been changed, to discard the old, embrace the new, and run headlong down an immutable course. It happened to me... on that summer's day, when my eyes were opened to the sea."
—Jacques Cousteau, Oceanographer

He conducted research using test samples from oceans all around the world in about 1936. Wonderfully, in ocean samples taken all over the globe, Dr. Murray personally always found the existence of 90 plus water soluble minerals and trace elements. This fact should not be too amazing as it certainly makes sense that all minerals found on land would be in the ocean. However, what was of special interest was just *how* these minerals were **perfectly blended and uniquely configured together into a wonderful life sustaining symphony**.

These minerals and trace elements that were found on Earth were uniquely blended into the *perfect and consistent nourishing* liquefied solution that allowed the ocean life to completely flourish. Whereas in our soil on land, there can be varying amounts and a different mineral and trace element package in one area of soil as compared to another area just a few feet away.

At the time of Dr. Murray's earlier research, **his findings revealed a seeming *absence* of deteriorating health and disease in the ocean life in unpolluted seawater**.

Can humans become healthier like sea animals if mineral needs of body are met?
Photograph by Al Alicea, AlAliceaPhotography.com.

He also noticed surprisingly that the aging process was not expressing itself as it did in land life. The astonishing findings on the superb health of the sea life caused Dr. Murray to passionately dedicate his life to learning more about the ocean's highly nourishing, health building, and health protective natural solution.

One could not help but wonder if this full and perfectly blended arrangement of 90 plus minerals and trace elements found in the ocean itself is the "perfect recipe" to promote land life as it appears to be for promoting the health of ocean life.

He was hoping he could help to resolve the many health challenges and diseases that could be resulting from mineral depleted soils and thus mineral depleted foods contributing to a breakdown in health—to bodies increasingly less capable of warding off disease and unwellness. He was determined to learn how the full spectrum of the ocean's magnificent nutrients could be best and most easily "transferred" to be used as a fertilizer for soil and crops, so the health of people could improve.

Wonderfully, Dr. Murray found great success actually using diluted seawater to grow a wide range of crops.

He found the oceanic nutrients helped remineralize soil in a safe and non-toxic way. He found the seawater was an abundant and sustainable source of nutrients for the soil and plants. *However*, he also recognized not everyone lived close to an ocean to access it phenomenal nutrients, and it was not practical to "bottle it up" and ship to those inland areas.

The limitation of access to the seawater for many, led to his wanting to "capture" the ocean's essence into a fertilizing product that could be more easily transported. And thus his perseverance paid off and "capture" the seawater's nutritive essence he did. He found very careful sun evaporation of the ocean solidified those precious liquid minerals....

In fact, with carefulness, 100% of minerals and trace elements in the ocean water came into the sea salt!

He referred to this sea salt as "sea solids" which are now are officially named SEA-90 sea solids. The name SEA-90 sea solids refers to the full array of 90 plus elements found in the sea solids, elements that are perfectly proportioned like those found in the ocean.

Dr. Murray found all elements on Earth are found in the dehydrated "sea solids" with possible exception of some of the gases.

Dr. Murray fertilized by using the sea solids in their hardened form. When water is added to soil where the sea solids are located, they dissolve. And he also used them by making a liquid fertilizer by simply adding water to them so they would dissolve. He used them for soil, gardens, crops, and even as a mineral source for livestock. He must have found much gratification in this.

Again, when the ocean water was properly and carefully solar evaporated, mineral rich grayish in color sea salt with the full array of minerals and trace elements was the result. Eureka! He termed this sea salt "sea solids" understanding there could be a *huge* difference in the mineral levels in different kinds of sea salt based on how it was harvested, where it was obtained, and how it was processed. He did testing on his "sea solids" to verify that the unique and full compilation of minerals in the ocean were indeed found in them.

In oceans around the world, they are always made up of 90 plus minerals and trace elements in the same configuration.
Photograph by Anne Landois-Favret.

Really, nothing compares to the mineral supremacy of the seawater. This briny formula not only contains all of the 90 plus minerals and trace

35

elements on Earth, but they are arranged in a brilliant particular order, with certain percentages of each mineral. These mineral percentages never change. They are *always* in constant relation and ratio to one another, even if the salinity (*total amount* of those elements) increase or decrease. It is the "management skills" of the ocean that maintain this flawless salty environment.

In 1865, Johan Georg Forchhammer found that regardless of variation in salinity, the ratio of major salts in samples of seawater from locations around the world was constant. (Remarkably, excess minerals fall to the bottom of the ocean.) This constant ratio of ocean elements is known as The Principle of Constant Proportions.

Aging Process Did Not Seem to Appear in Sea Animals Immersed in Salty Ocean Fluid

Once more, Dr. Murray was tremendously impressed by the high disease resistance of animals in the sea—especially as compared to those on land. At the time, he noted the *shocking* absence of disease in the sea and also the wonderful vitality of the sea animals.

Seawater contains every existing mineral in liquid form.

He theorized that land life had more disease from consuming mineral depleted and weaker plants from mineral deficient soils. Dr. Murray said.

"There is no chronic disease to be found among fish and animal life in the sea that compares to those on land."

This exemplary researcher, who also had a passion for growing plants hydroponically, noted the aging process did not seem to appear or exist with the sea animals he studied.

Dr. Murray found sea turtles with amazingly good health.

For example, at the time of his research, he was surprisingly unable to find cancer, hardening of the arteries, or arthritis in sea turtles in the pure and untainted ocean—with its smorgasbord of naturally balanced minerals. Dr. Murray imparted.

"It is also known that all land animals develop arteriosclerosis, yet sea animals have never been diagnosed as arteriosclerotic."

This unique humanitarian believed that *all* minerals and trace elements found in the impressive ocean—a bountiful treasure chest, are *all* necessary, *in some way*, to our physiological well-being, our immune systems, and our mental health.

Again, Dr. Murray envisioned sea energy agriculture being a solution to a looming crisis in agriculture and food production.

Chapter 5: Superior Form of Fertilization to Replenish Our Soil

"Not yet, however, have we recognized soil fertility as the food producing forces within the soil that reveal national and international patterns of weakness and strength."

—Dr. Weston A. Price
Nutrition and Physical Degeneration

How Can We be Largely Blinded to the Fertilization Gifts of the Ocean Minerals?

First, here is a little fun science to help you understand our interconnectedness with sea salt, and to appreciate the value of sea salt as a fertilizer.

Scientists believe liquid water began accumulating on the surface of the Earth about 4 billion years ago, forming the early ocean. There is evidence of microscopic life later in the seas about 3.4 billion years ago, with other bigger life forms evolving from the ocean to the land millions of years ago.

The ancient salty seas covered *most* of the surface of the Earth, exposing very little land. These ancient salty seas were believed to be even saltier than the oceans of today. Estimates of the salinity range of the early oceans was between 1.2 to 2 times our present day average ocean salinity levels.

Salt Content of Seawater VS Human Blood	
Sea Water	Human Blood
Appx. 3.5%	Appx. 1% (0.9)
The body contains the 0.9% salty "sea water" within its internal fluids: tears, saliva, sweat, amniotic fluid, cell cytoplasm, etc.	

Today, our oceans are an average of 35 parts per thousand (ppt) salinity which means 35 pounds of salt per 1,000 pounds of sea water—about 3.5% salt. Human blood contains about 0.9 percent salt—almost 1% salt.

Also now, about 71% of the earth is covered by oceans well seasoned with salt. About 80 percent of all life on Earth is found in the salty, life-sustaining oceans. Estimations indicate if the abundant salt in the oceans could be removed and spread evenly over the Earth's land surface, it would form a layer more than 500 feet (166 meters) thick, plenty of salt to be used for gardens and farming!

The Hidden Secret to Sea Salt as a Highly Effective Fertilizer is Having the Right Salinity Level

Different plants prefer different salinity levels, or different amounts of salt in the soil. In agriculture, too high a degree of salinization interferes with the growth of all but those plants specifically adapted for it. On the other hand, with the right amount of sea salt, many plants can *absolutely* flourish.

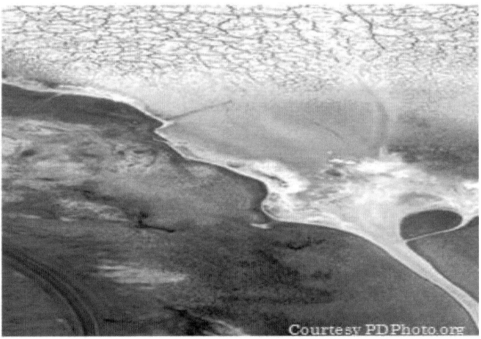
Too high a concentration of sea salt and crops won't grow.

After natural catastrophes like tsunamis, widespread crop damage can occur from the onslaught of ocean salt. However, some farmers have been happily surprised to learn the recovery of the soil (the right salinity level from later dispersed and rain-diluted ocean salt) allowed for new crops to successfully grow again in a far shorter time than anticipated. In fact, after the 2004 tsunami in Indonesia, they found the salty fertilizer **_doubled_ their rice yield and other crops truly thrived**.

The full variety of sea salt minerals are _perfectly_ balanced and have not been manipulated by man.

In Japan, after the ravaging 2011 tsunami, farmers found the salty soil to be *ideal* for growing cotton. When crops are fertilized with a *full* spectrum of sea minerals that represent the "heart of the ocean," it is remarkably discovered that a wide variety of plants do *exceptionally* well and produce mineral rich crops that have **_increased resistance_ to disease**. Fortunately, sea mineral farming is slowly gaining attention.

Every Single Form of Life on Our Planet *Requires* Salt to Survive

Salt beds or deposits on land resulted from evaporated ancient seas—trapped when land masses arose from the oceans. When the ocean water evaporates, the minerals solidify. **This *unprocessed* sea salt contains all the elements supporting life.**

Dried salt beds remain from evaporated ancient seas.

The needed "ingredients" for the ocean to *precisely* make its health promoting saline "soup" come from different sources:

- Over the believed billions of years, eroded mineral rocks, mountains, and the Earth's crust have been transported to the sea from rains and streams
- Gaseous components released from the Earth's crust through volcanic openings or that came from the atmosphere
- Superheated water, rich with dissolved minerals gushing through hydrothermal vents in the bottom of the oceans
- Volcanoes erupting hot rock under the ocean which dissolves

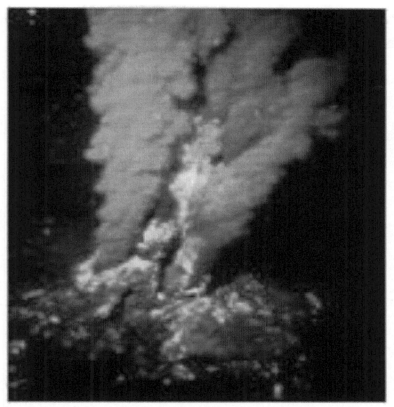

Hydrothermal vent discharges mineral rich water, and bacteria flourish around these vents.

Salt is the only rock eaten by human beings. **It is an instrumental source of nutrients needed for humans and animals to live.** And animals need more salt than people. In fact, many formerly created roads were simply widened trails that were originally created by animals in search of salt licks. Villages were started at the end of such trails in order to have a nearby supply of their *essential-for-living* salt.

A wild heard of Indian bison enjoy a natural salt lick in Rajiv Gandhi National Park in Southern India.

Photograph by Amog Rajenderan.

Giraffe is licking artificial salt lick in the Pilanesberg Game Reserve, South Africa.

Reindeer (caribou) licking salt that was used to de-ice roadway in British Columbia.

Three Bighorn sheep discover a natural salt lick along Guanella Pass, a few miles south of Georgetown, Colorado.

Continuing, in the past, in every century and on each continent, the predominant people were the ones that were in control of the potentially lucrative salt trade. Many *extremely powerful* salt empires were built.

Numerous fascinating methods were and are used around the world to gather this *essential* commodity.

Salt mine in New York.

Salt is being carried away.

The salt pools of Maras, Peru operate from the Pre-Inca time. They are traditionally available to any person wishing to harvest salt.

Scraped salt put into piles in Uyuni, Bolivia ready to be hauled away. There are higher and lower grades of salt used in different ways.
Photograph by Alicia Nijdam.

Salt extraction pools in Las Salinas Grandes, a huge high-altitude salt desert in Argentina's northwest.
Photograph by Nils Rinaldi.

Harvesting sea salt in Poitou-Charentes, France.
Photograph by Didier Hannot.

We Carry the "Sea" Within Us, Non-Refined Sea Salt is Our Friend

Of further interest, a healthy adult body contains about 250 grams of salt. This amount would fill three salt shakers. Since our bodies continually lose salt through our functions and activities, the lost salt supply needs to be continually replaced. Salt is necessary for the delivery of nutrients, the transmitting of electrical nerve impulses, and the contractions of the heart and other muscles. Sea salt elements promote respiratory health, blood sugar health, sinus health, bone strength, plus so much more.

On average, there are three salt shakers worth of salt in each adult.

Additionally, scientists believe all plant cells evolved from ancient salty oceans. Surviving and flourishing in such a briny environment dates back to these earliest plants. Understanding how indispensible unrefined sea salt is to *living* organisms should help us *easily* understand the incredible value it can play in farming and gardening.

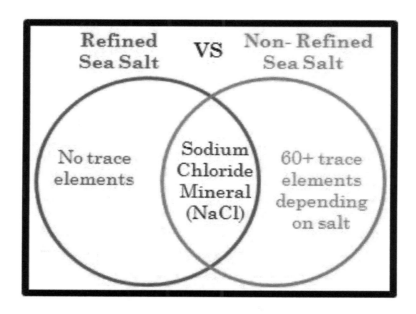

Importantly, the sea denizens *perfectly* sustained in the pure ocean are *not* sustained by water and *refined* salt. They thrive as a result of the perfect chemistry of the ocean.

Wheat Plant Flourishes With Sea Solids Fertilization

Sea mineral fertilization can support the wheat plant on land—the very wheat plant that so generously supplies the wheat seeds for growing young wheatgrass. Beneficial microbes feast on the sea solids and then increase in population, *further* enriching the soil.

"All the problems inherent in our modern system can be eliminated with the application of Sea Energy in Agriculture and good sense in Processing."
—Dr. Maynard Murray

SEA-90 sea solids fertilizer has been successfully used for enhancing the growth of wheat fields in Nebraska. Charles Walters, author of *Fertility from the Ocean Deep,* shares the testimony of a Nebraska farmer who found his wheat crop grew in stronger, fuller, and matured earlier….

"That wheat was the best wheat I ever grew. It came out of the soil. It covered the hill like hair on a dog's back."

Regarding sea solids fertilizer for wheat, Walters also mentions…

"Used in wheat fields in selenium or molybdenum excess areas, sea solids seem to govern uptake of the excess, making the wheat commercially useable on otherwise condemned acres."

Sea Minerals Eco-Fertilizer Benefits Soil, Plants, Animals, and Humans

Dr. Murray reasoned that if the sea environment could maintain such a high level of disease resistance and be highly supportive of sea *life*, then perhaps plants on land could also greatly benefit. His reasoning was sound….

By properly harvesting sea mineral solids from the ocean, and using those unrefined sea solids as a soil amendment, he found he could *most definitely* bestow the fertility and health promoting legacy of the ocean to plants on land as well.

He personally experienced *profound* success growing plants that were fertilized with sea solids. In fact, as his research continued, he captivatingly found that not only did the sea solids fertilized plants benefit, but the animals fortunate enough to eat those mineral rich foods experienced very desirable health improvements as well.

SEA-90 sea solids are drying in foreground and are formed during solar evaporation. Dissolved salts (elements) crystallize out of the liquid ocean.
Photograph by SeaAgri.com.

Remineralization with a Full Spectrum of the Ocean's Minerals in Sea Solids Leads to Many Exceptional Benefits

Plants Benefit
- Plants flourished
- Increased disease resistance—predators are drawn to weaker, malnourished plants
- Improved crop yields
- Less need for other fertilizers, insecticides, fungicides, herbicides
- Improved taste, sweeter tasting from increased plant sugars
- Faster growth
- Healthier
- Longer shelf life
- Increased protein in alfalfa

Animals Benefit From Eating Plants Fertilized with Sea Minerals
- Chickens exhibited perfect health
- Improved reproduction and fertility
- Improved immunity
- Increased disease resistance
- Steers showed weight gain while eating less food (appreciated in farming)
- Animals delighted in salted crop fields
- Exhibited more shiny, lush, sleek coats
- More calm, less nervous
- Increased protein, butterfat in livestock

Chapter 6: Research on Positive Impact of Foods Fertilized with Good Sea Salt

"I have used these sea solids as plant food in experiments to prove that these elements in perfect balance will grow chemically perfect plants.

"Note that I did not try to synthesize anything, but merely took what nature already offered."

—Maynard Murray, M.D.
Sea Energy Agriculture

Cancer Bred Mice Doubled Their Life Span With Good Sea Salt Mineral Fertilized Foods

Dr. Murray conducted feeding experiments using sea mineral solids fertilized foods with C3H mice that carried the MMTV, and with rats. (C3H mice are used in research because they always (100%) develop breast cancer, and MMTV stands for mouse mammary tumor virus.)

He made it clear these experiments were conducted on C3H mice and rats, and not humans. Nevertheless, the impressive results indicated a possible way to increase disease resistance and improve health for humans through sea solids fertilized agriculture, and begged for further research. Following, are two of his studies.

In one study, he decided to work with 400 female C3H mice specifically bred to develop breast cancer which would bring about their demise. He broke the C3H mice into two groups—200 mice in each group. One control group was fed regular foods and the other experimental group was fed foods fertilized with sea solids. The control group of mice all died within eight months and seven days (they have a life expectancy of *no more* than nine months). The experimental mice that were fed foods fertilized with unprocessed sea solids with attached minerals and trace elements **all lived until they were sacrificed at 16 months:**

Testing Showed No Cancerous Tissue at That Time.

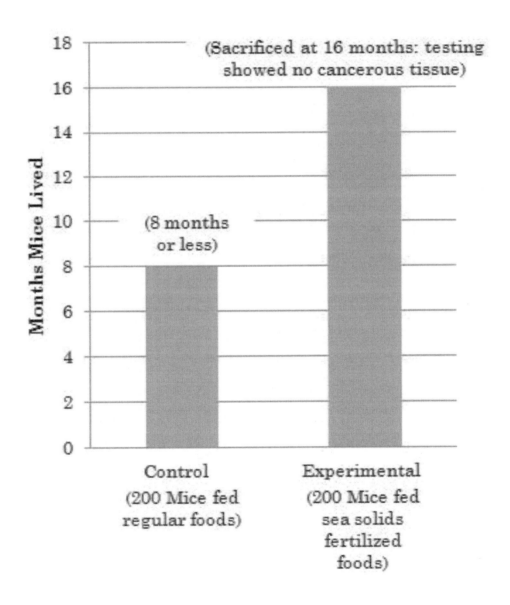

Life Span Doubled for Cancer Bred C3H Mice Fed Sea Solids Fertilized Foods

Months Mice Lived

(Sacrificed at 16 months: testing showed no cancerous tissue)

(8 months or less)

Control (200 Mice fed regular foods)

Experimental (200 Mice fed sea solids fertilized foods)

Rats Injected With Cancer Lived Longer With Foods Remineralized From Good Sea Salt

Dr. Murray also experimented with 50 Sprague Dolly rats. All of the rats were injected with cancer (Jensen Carcino-Sarcoma) —shown to be 100% fatal. He then divided the 50 rats into two groups of 25. The control rats were fed regular food, while the experimental rats were fed sea mineral solids fertilized food.

All the rats eating regular foods perished within 21 days. Nine of the rats in the experimental group fed sea mineral solids fertilized foods lived 19 days longer, for 40 days. The remaining 16 experimental rats (64%) were sacrificed at 150 days or 5 months, and found to be cancer free. These results were nothing short of amazing.

This is huge! The more mineral and trace elements in the soil, the more in the food, and the more disease resistant the mice!

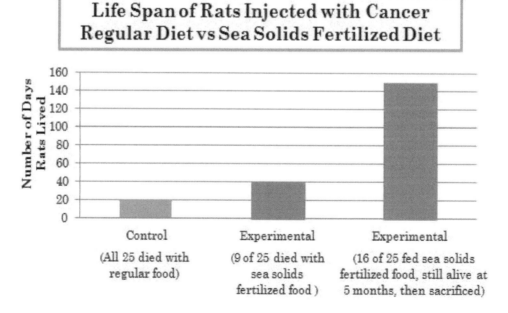

Life Span of Rats Injected with Cancer
Regular Diet vs Sea Solids Fertilized Diet

60

Chapter 7: Which Plants Love Sea Salt Fertilization?

"Dr. William Albrecht of the Department of Agriculture at the University of Missouri used to say, 'Disease preys on an undernourished plant.' I say, 'Disease preys on an undernourished body.' "

—Dr. Bernard Jensen

Other Plants Also Thrive With Sea Salt Solution

As mentioned, my wheatgrass thrived when fertilized with sea salt. Over the course of a few years, I experimented with several different sea salts on the market. My wheatgrass did especially well with the SEA-90 sea solids. It was interesting to me that when tasting the different sea salts I was experimenting with, the SEA-90 sea solids tasted the most like the ocean itself.

It was fun when I realized *numerous* other plants *love* salty sea solid minerals from the ocean too, and I continue to experiment with them at home. Fertilizing with sea solids is not an exact science, but there are recommended application guidelines for fertilizing different plants, and those recommendations can be found at SeaAgri.com. You can also purchase sea solids there.

Wheatgrass as well as many other plants thrive when being fertilized with the abundant and sustainable sea salt.

Keep in mind, plants cannot absorb elements from the soil unless they are in *liquid* form—and sea salt is *100%* soluble (*fully* liquefying and dissolving when water is mixed with them) and are available for *immediate* plant uptake.

Non-refined sea salt is simple to use, affordable, sustainable, earth-friendly, easy to store, and a *highly productive* way to provide a complete assortment of elements to the grateful grass and other plants. When you drink juice from this wheatgrass or eat foods grown in this soil, you will take in their storehouse of replenishing nutrients.

It is indeed fact that the naturally proportioned, perfectly balanced chemistry of minerals and trace elements found in the good sea salt, are not only clearly optimal for the growth and nourishment of sea vegetation and other sea life but *also* for land life. I recommend SEA-90 sea solids as a safe and natural fertilizer. **Again, when sea solids are combined with water, and thus dissolved, their elements are *instantly* available for plant uptake.**

Many plants flourish with whole, non-refined, mineral and trace element rich sea salt or sea solids fertilization. Again, microorganisms in the soil feast on sea minerals and flourish. Following are a few plants that grow quite well in this nutrient rich healthier soil.

Chapter 8: How Do I Select Good Sea Salt?

"Every disease is a sign of a lack of certain chemical elements. No disease can exist unless there is a lack of chemical elements in the body."

—Bernard Jensen
The Healing Power of Chlorophyll from Plant Life

Is All Sea Salt Equal? No

Is there a difference in the quality of different solid sea salts being marketed for farming and gardens? Yes, there is absolutely a difference. As mentioned, the way in which the sea salt is harvested and processed will impact the true amount of minerals and trace elements in the salt. Ideally, you want grayish colored sea salt—more indicative of the entire mineral and trace element package from the ocean. And ideally, a mineral analysis sheet (if available) on the particular sea salt will help you pick your best options.

SEA-90 sea solids at SeaAgri.com are listed by the USDA National Organic Program and the Organic Materials Review Institute (OMRI) for use in the production of organic food, fiber, and livestock.

You certainly do not want to use refined, element depleted sea salt as a fertilizer. The more naturally proportioned minerals in your non-refined sea salt fertilizer, as found in the ocean, the better. Huge differences exist between different salts as communicated in the salt comparison chart I'll present in a bit. Remember, the more minerals and trace elements in your sea salt, the more that will be available for the plant to extract. You can then be assured the minerals and trace elements your plant desires will be available for its uptake.

If you are unable to obtain the SEA-90, look for another sea salt that is unrefined, with off-white, grayish, beige or tan coloring (not white), and that was harvested from the fresh ocean—ideally, where rainfall has not washed away any of the valuable elements. And sea salt mined from land or below the surface of the Earth can have lost elements through various ways, or be higher in certain elements like iron for example, thus not preserving that sought after perfect arrangement of all elements as found in the ocean. Also, learn as much about the sea salt company as you can to understand their harvesting methods—you want as many minerals and trace elements as possible best capturing the entire nourishing synergy of the ocean.

Unrefined sea salt mounds in Bolivia have natural grayish hue.
Photograph by Luca Galuzzi.

You can certainly mix-and-match your fertilizer choices for gardening. You can use your other fertilizer choices *along with* the sea solids. If you want an outstanding ocean based fertilizer that is affordable, highly valuable, safe, easy to store, simple to apply, and 100% soluble, I absolutely recommend using the SEA-90 sea solids.

Off-white crystal sea solids grains have their own unique shape and size. No minerals or trace elements have been removed, leached, or weathered away from them.

According to Dr. Murray, there is no sea salt available anywhere that compares to the SEA-90 sea mineral solids harvested at the special and pristine location he discovered. He searched the planet and found only three perfect locations where he knew he could obtain and diligently harvest sea solids to preserve their buffet of minerals and trace elements—the foundation for life.

If you use other sea salt besides the SEA-90 sea solids, you will not be getting the entire mineral and trace elements and biological package, and your results will vary.

Ocean water is a highly nutritional liquid largely responsible for the near perfection of the ocean creatures and plants within. The sea plants within this fluid are *byproducts* of the ocean and contain different amounts and proportions of minerals within them. Sea foods are absolutely *highly* nutritious and tremendously valuable to us. However, the seawater "mother" of these byproducts must be recognized for her mineral abundant superiority—her *unequaled, fully complete,* and *unique* mineral package.

Side Note: Could this be why wheatgrass juice is fantastic for feeding and nourishing the body? **As grass is the *only* plant that can absorb every single mineral and trace element that is in the soil.** And as mentioned earlier, a *wide* variety of minerals, even if only available in minuscule amounts, are *essential* to the *proper* functioning of man.

Ocean water is a highly nutritional liquid largely responsible for the near perfection of the ocean creatures and plants within. The sea plants within this fluid are *byproducts* of the ocean and contain different amounts and proportions of minerals within them. Sea foods are absolutely *highly* nutritious and tremendously valuable to us. However, the seawater "mother" of these byproducts must be recognized for her mineral abundant superiority—her *unequaled, fully complete,* and *unique* mineral package.

Again, this phenomenal seawater recipe contains *every single* mineral and trace element on Planet Earth, a *precise* bit of this mineral and a *precise* bit of that mineral. In all oceans around the world, there is always a constant ratio of these seawater minerals to one another. As the *concentration* of salinity of the seawater can increase or decrease, these oceanic minerals *always* maintain their "one of a kind" and *fixed proportions* to each other—while they can *overall* increase or decrease in abundance. This unique and salubrious orchestration of naturally occurring 90 plus minerals and trace elements constitute our wondrous oceans. Give glory to the Creator!

Please realize, **unprocessed ocean salt is far different in composition and more life giving than the majority of refined mineral depleted salt on the market today**. The valuable minerals and trace elements can be stripped from the sea salt during processing and sold to the supplements industry. Please see my Salt Comparison Charts to help you determine the best quality sea salt.

The more minerals in the sea salt, and the more its mineral compilation *is in line* with that in the ocean, the better it is for fertilization. You want the salt to duplicate the ocean's salty chemical arrangement *as much as possible*. There are many different ways to process sea salt, and each method can produce a *very* chemically different sea salt end product. There can be *vast* differences in quality between the different sea salts on the market. When it comes to sea salt, the more identical it is in mineral composition to the sea, the most natural it is. It really is hard to improve upon the genius of Mother Nature.

All Salt Originates From the Sea - A Salt Comparison Chart

	Refined Salt
Ingredients	Sodium Chloride plus additives which can include: anti-caking agents, bleaching agents, aluminum derivates, sugar, fluoride, potassium iodide. (Additives do not need to be on label.) 93% used for industrial purposes, remaining used in food business, especially preservative in processed foods
Color and shape	White; small grain for easy pouring
Located	Salt mines on land or ocean
Processing method	Varies
Element status	Elements are stripped and sold to industry
Notes	Can be referred to as white poison; inflammatory, unnatural, unwholesome food

	Unrefined Salt
Ingredients	Sodium chloride along with accompanied elements, read label for any additives * I select unrefined sea salts for seasoning my foods, preferring gray, sun dehydrated sea salt from fresh ocean water to best retain minerals and elements in balanced proportion as found in ocean, with no additives, tested for pollutants.
Color and shape	Usually white, pinkish, or gray. Black or red sea salts can get their color from added activated charcoal, or red clay; grain size varies
Located	Salt mines on land or ocean
Processing method	Varies
Element status	Some elements can be missing depending on processing method and where obtained, or could have been rinsed or weathered away
Notes	Can be referred to as white gold; anti-inflammatory, healing, natural, nourishing

	SEA-90 Sea Solids
Ingredients	Sodium chloride along with accompanied 90+ balanced minerals and trace elements—no additives, tested for pollutants * Ideal for wheatgrass growing and gardening (when combined with water, the elements become isotonic and *immediately* available for plant to absorb)
Color and shape	Tan or gray – Off-white color indicates retaining of darker trace elements; grain size varies
Located	Ocean
Processing method	Sun dehydrated and harvested from fresh seawater
Element status	Care is taken to best capture *all* balanced elements in ocean, sea solids protected from rains rinsing away valuable elements
Notes	Harvested from sea to capture complete spectrum of minerals and trace elements for fertilization

Simple Recipe for Making Sea Salt Liquid Fertilizer

It is simple to make a SEA-90 sea solids and water solution, or a sea salt and water solution to be used as a liquid fertilizer. A little of the sea solids go a long way. Each time I watered my wheatgrass, I used the sea solids liquid fertilizer—like diluted seawater. Sea solids can also be used in their natural solid form and placed in soil. When soil is watered, the sea solids easily dissolve.

For sea solids recommended applications and instructions for various plants, go to SeaAgri.com. If you cannot obtain the SEA-90 sea solids garden fertilizer which is the best choice and that is *superb,* you can use an ocean harvested sea salt as explained next.

You are certainly welcome to experiment with different proportions and salinity levels, but the following liquid fertilizer recipe works quite well for wheatgrass and other plants. **Do not use refined, mineral and trace element depleted salt.**

Fertilizer Recipe

Mix 1 Gallon of Water With 1 Teaspoon SEA-90 Sea Solids

(Or other ocean harvested sea salt with full spectrum of minerals and trace elements)

Recommended Ocean Based Fertilizers

1. SEA-90 Sea Solids at SeaAgri.com – Perfect for wheatgrass

2. Well selected non-refined sea salt harvested from fresh seawater that best preserves the full spectrum of minerals and trace elements

SEA-90 sea solids are a superior natural and sustainable fertilizer.

Stir the SEA-90 sea solids and water together until the grains dissolve—the *larger* particles from the grains *may* require several hours or overnight to dissolve—especially if using a larger salty grain like SEA-90 sea solids.

With SEA-90 sea solids, any residue still existing is both non-liquefying rock dust and crystals too large to quickly liquefy.

Chapter 9: Did Sea Salt Cause Caterpillars to Leave Plant?

"Soil biology conserves fertility, and any 'fertilizer' that kills off soil biology does not deserve to be called a fertilizer."

—Charles Walters

Caterpillars Do Not Like Eating Grapevine Leaves Sprayed with Sea Salt and Water Solution

You will have fun experimenting with this sea salt and water solution and observing firsthand how it helps you to grow better plants that are more pest and disease resistant.

There is a grapevine growing on the fence between my house and my neighbors. While walking by the grapevine one day, I was shocked to find literally hundreds of hungry caterpillars devouring the leaves like little Pac-Men hurriedly moving eastbound from right to left along the vine. I had never seen anything like it and my first thought was to save the rest of the remaining leaves.

I had read that some people using sea solids found the use of other fertilizers, pesticides, and herbicides to be often unnecessary. Their crops not only thrived, but they better resisted insects and disease.

Also, in my *How to Grow Glorious Wheatgrass at Home Tutorial*, I teach how to foliar feed wheatgrass (spray leaves with the sea salt and water solution) and I explain the benefits. I wondered if foliar feeding the remaining grapevine leaves would somehow benefit the plant so the caterpillars would not eat the remaining green leaves.

But I also thought it might be too late to save those last few uneaten leaves. The caterpillars were fast eaters, and I thought with hundreds of caterpillars on the leaves, I may not find much luck with my "safe for the environment" sea salt spray.

Earlier in the day, I proceeded anyway and I took out my sprayer container in which I had my sea solids and water solution (**1 tsp. sea solids per 1 gallon water**) and sprayed the remaining few green leaves in the grapevine. I sprayed the leaves on the top surface primarily. If I could, I sprayed on the underside of the leaf too. There were caterpillars on those remaining green leaves and I just sprayed right on top of them. It only took a minute or so to spray what little leaves were remaining. I then continued to go about my day.

I recommend sprayers at my website HealthBanquet.com. Following is me foliar feeding my wheatgrass with the sprayer. I used this sprayer to also spray the grapevine leaves.

Wheatgrass being sprayed with whole sea solids and water liquid fertilizer.

Following is a wide picture of the grapevine and its green grapes on a cloudy day. The brown devoured leaves you see are what were left after being mostly eaten by the caterpillars.

Grapevine plant on fence. Caterpillars eating leaves from right to left side. May 27, 2012.

Closer view of the eaten leaves. May 27, 2012.

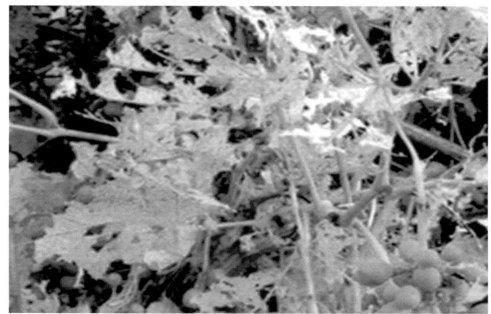

Further close-up of eaten grapevine leaves. May 27, 2012.

Remaining green leaves are circled above. May 27, 2012

Caterpillars were found mostly on the underside of the leaves. May 27, 2012.

Close-up of caterpillars on leaves. May 27, 2012.

I took a peek at the leaves later in the day after my first spraying, but really could not tell if some of the caterpillars had decided to leave and stop eating the remaining leaves. I could tell where I had sprayed, as after the water had evaporated from the leaf, there was a slight white film or white salt residue on the surface of the leaf.

The next day I looked again, and guess what? I could definitely tell the formerly hungry caterpillars had slowed down in their eating. Now, there were still caterpillars on the leaves, but their eating patterns had decreased dramatically!

At the speed the caterpillars were eating the leaves prior to my spraying them, the remaining leaves would have been munched away to about nothing by the next day. But because of the sea salt spraying, this was not the case. Marvelously, the next day, I think just about all of the leaves were still there and still intact. **The caterpillars decided to just about totally stop eating them!**

I decided to give the leaves another foliar spray with the sea salt and water solution simply because it was so easy to do. I don't know if that extra spray was necessary for "natural pest resistance" but it was so easy to do, I just sprayed them again.

Day after day, the remaining leaves were still largely unharmed, and uneaten! Again, there were a few remaining caterpillars left on the leaves, eating perhaps just a *tiny* bit, but most had left. It seemed the caterpillars did not like eating leaves that had been sprayed with the sea salt and water solution.

Maybe they ate a little of the "salted" leaves and then just could not tolerate the salt. Was it because the sea salt is a desiccant and too drying for the caterpillars? I don't know exactly *why* they stopped eating them. But I do know the sea salt solution deterred them from eating the remaining leaves of this grapevine plant. It was amazing really and very exciting for me!

I immediately imagined how this sea salt and water solution could assist in the farming and gardening arena as a smart way to help reduce pests in a safe, non-toxic way. As unfortunately, there are estimated to be over 5 billion pounds of hazardous pesticides applied to crops annually in the United States, deadly chemicals that poison our environment—upon which we all depend for our survival. There must be a better way, and I believe Sea Salt Fertilization can lead us to a better way.

"The chemicals to which life is asked to make its adjustment are no longer merely the calcium and silica and copper and all the rest of the minerals washed out of the rocks and carried in rivers to the sea; they are the synthetic creations of man's inventive mind, brewed in his laboratories, and having no counterparts in nature....

"These sprays, dusts, and aerosols are now applied almost universally to farms, gardens, forest, and homes—nonselective chemicals that have the power to kill every insect, the "good" and the "bad," to still the song of birds and the leaping of fish in the streams, to coat the leaves with a deadly film, and to linger on in soil—all this though the intended target may be only a few weeds or insects. Can anyone believe it is possible to lay down such a barrage of poisons on the surface of Earth without making it unfit for all life? They should not be called "insecticides," but "biocides."
—Rachel Carson
Silent Spring

Good sea salt is safe for the plant, easy to apply, safe for those applying the solution, and affordable. I look forward to the day more people become aware of the great potential for this saline solution and Sea Salt Fertilization to deter pests from plants.

To continue, four days later the green leaves were still basically the same. There were a few caterpillars remaining on the leaves, but their leaf consumption had definitely decreased if not stopped entirely.

Green leaves on left side of grapevine are still intact four days later.
May 31, 2012

Sea salt solution deterred the caterpillars. Fully intact green leaves
are still there. Fantastic!
May 31. 2012.

As time passed, eventually the caterpillars completely left and they did not return. I believe they went to go look for a more "non-salted" food source.

I knew of the antibacterial and antifungal properties of non-refined sea salt complete with its full spectrum of minerals and trace elements. I knew the sea salt solution was a champion fertilizing agent for wheatgrass and other plants, and helped plants become more disease resistant. But I never could have imagined the leaves sprayed with the sea salt solution would so *quickly* cause a *dramatic* shift in the eating habits of the caterpillars. It was really something to witness this.

In conclusion, I believe good mineral rich sea salt has *tremendous* potential to deter pests and help prevent plant disease, in addition to its many other *unmatched* nourishing qualities. And as you have seen in the science experiments I have presented, *extraordinary* things can happen through the consumption of truly mineral-abundant "sea salt" fertilized foods.

My wish is that you have enjoyed the "sea salt as fertilizer" information I have presented—information I learned simply because I was *initially* just seeking a solution to grow healthier wheatgrass. I hope I have opened your eyes to the many benefits of Sea Salt Fertilization, and you shall be encouraged to try it in your gardening.

The son of one of my good friends did a classroom science experiment showing how sea salt can be used to successfully fertilize wheatgrass. Maybe you have some good ideas on how to get the word out on Sea Salt Fertilization too.

Wheatgrass fertilized with good sea salt.

Let's use Sea Salt Fertilization to help minimize the usage of dangerous chemicals being sprayed on our soil and plants—toxic and hormone disrupting chemicals that are throwing our delicate hormonal systems "out of whack," harming us as well as our ecosystem. Let's use Sea Salt Fertilization to remineralize our soil and grow *truly* mineral rich plants.

The using of the right kind of sea salt in your gardening will ensure *each and every one* of the precious and life supporting planetary minerals and trace elements, that your plants would like to absorb, will now be available for easy assimilation. No more mineral depleted soil!

With emphasis, please spread the good news on this revolutionary topic to your farming and gardening friends and those that care about the environment and our health—to create a tectonic shift in our fertilization practices.

I shall continue to experiment with sea salt with the full spectrum of minerals and trace elements in my gardening. And I hope one day in the future when we shop at the store or farmer's market, we will see foods labeled as "Sea Salt Fertilized" or "Seawater Fertilized." I optimistically await that day.

Furthermore, it is good to reflect upon the fascinating anti-aging qualities of the marine life fortunate enough to absorb the ocean's essence and consume a selection of health building sea mineral rich foods. Similarly, in terms of humans and of utmost significance, it is also highly advantageous *for us* to take in and consume mineral abundant foods to strengthen and comprehensively fortify our bodies and *support our ocean within*, to enhance our health as well!

Realize, most people are not *yet* aware that the ancient ocean is a vast reservoir of *unsurpassed* sea nutrients that can greatly benefit humankind. *You* now have this knowledge. Therefore, you understand *why* it is especially wise to strengthen your interconnectedness and relationship with the nutritive ocean, and its non-refined, mineral rich salt.

All things considered, I hope you will have a deeper appreciation and respect for the almighty ocean when you visit the beach. And very importantly, we need to do what we can to protect our irreplaceable oceans, as God may not have another brilliant and perfect solution to supremely nourish our soil, plants, and therefore us.

References and Resources

Batmanghelidj, F. *Obesity Cancer Depression, Their Common Cause & Natural Cure*. Falls Church, VA: Global Health Solutions, Inc., 2004.

Brummit, Chris, "Tsunami Actually Aided Crops in Indonesia." USAToday.com, September 26, 2005. http://www.usatoday.com/news/world/2005—09—25—tsunami—crops_x .htm.

Hendel, Barbara, Peter Ferreira. *Water & Salt, The Essence of Life*. Switzerland: Gymona Holding AG, 2002.

Landais, Emmanuelle. "Researchers Explore Ways to Use Sea Water for Farming." Gulfnews.com, Nov. 23, 2010. http://gulfnews.com/news/gulf/uae/environment/researchers—explore—w ays—to—use—sea—water—for—farming—1.711262.

Langre, Jacques de. *Sea Salt's Hidden Powers*. Asheville, NC: Happiness Press, 1994.

Moyer, Melinda W. "It's Time to End the War on Salt," *Scientific American*, July 8, 2011. http://www.scientificamerican.com/article.cfm?id=its—time—to—end—t he—war—on—salt.

Mullen, Leslie. "Salt of the Early Earth," *Astrobiology Magazine*, June 11, 2001. http://www.astrobio.net/exclusive/223/salt—of—the—early—earth.

Murray, Maynard. *Sea Energy Agriculture, Perfect Natural Nutrition?* Winston—Salem, NC: Valentine Books, 1976.

Newcastle University. "Ancient Oceans Offer New Insight Into Origins of Animal Life," ScienceDaily. September 9, 2009. http://www.sciencedaily.com/releases/2009/09/090909133020.htm.

Ocean Health — http://www.oceanplasma.org/.

Ocean Solution Mineralizer – http://www.oceansolution.com/.

"Oldest Fossils Reveal Life 3.4 Billion Years Ago," *CBCNews, Technology and Science*. August 22, 2011. http://www.cbc.ca/news/technology/story/2011/08/22/science—oldest—fossils—bacteria—sulphur.html.

SeaAgri, Inc. SEA-90 100% Natural Sea Mineral Solids—Soil, Crop, and Livestock Nutrients from the Sea. http://www.seaagri.com/.

The Seawater Foundation. Sea water farming. http://www.seawaterfoundation.org.

University of California – Davis. "When the Earth Dried Out," *ScienceDaily*, February 8, 2002. http://www.sciencedaily.com/releases/2002/02/020208075438.htm.

Villemez, Jason, "Cotton Replaces Rice in Japan's Salt-Soaked Fields." PBS Newshour, September 16, 2011. http://www.pbs.org/newshour/updates/world/july—dec11/cotton_09—16.html.

Walters, Charles. *Fertility From The Ocean Deep, Nature's Perfect Nutrient Blend For The Farm*. Austin, TX: 2005.

Young, Gordon. The Essence of Life—Salt. *National Geographic*, September 1977, Page 381—401.

To Healthier Soil and a Healthier You!

Visit the Author

www.healthbanquet.com
www.facebook.com/healthbanquet
www.twitter.com/healthbanquet

Please spread the word and leave a review at Amazon.

Also by Eryn Paige

How to Grow Glorious Wheatgrass at Home Tutorial - With Salty Sea Mineral Eco-Fertilization for Superior Mineral Rich Soil

How and Why to Make Divine Soaked Flour Bread – For Easier Digestion and Optimized Nutrition

Closing Quote

"You can trace every sickness, every disease, and every ailment to a mineral deficiency."

—Linus Pauling, MD
Winner of two Nobel prizes

Made in the USA
San Bernardino, CA
08 February 2014